THE NEWEST FLOWER

written by
Juliese Y. Padgett

illustrated by
Remko Killaars

edited by
Jennifer Padgett

ISBN 978-1-63575-855-9 (Paperback)
ISBN 978-1-63575-857-3 (Hard Cover)
ISBN 978-1-63575-856-6 (Digital)

Christian Faith Publishing, Inc.
296 Chestnut Street
Meadville, PA 16335
www.christianfaithpublishing.com

Printed in the United States of America

Dedication

- Thank you, Lord, for giving me my forever family who has always been by my side! Mom, you will always be my beloved teacher!
- And to my favorite illustrator, Remko! I am amazed of how you made these characters come to life, just like my imagination! Without you and your family, this book would not be so beautiful, like a flower garden!
- May all the flowers in the world, including you, the reader, find the true Gardener to help them blossom!

Children's Challenge: See how many living creatures you can find in this book!

Acknowledgements

- My dream of helping orphans, like I once was, has finally come true! I am so thankful for the cheerleaders in my life: my dad, Jake, Jonah, Joelle, Uncle Nathanael, and my grandparents. Each has encouraged, guided, and believed in us during this book process.
- To my Mechanic Falls Vineyard family who has blessed us from the very beginning and helped both my sister and I get adopted.
- A very sincere thank you to our generous book sponsors:

1. The Maine Children's Home for Little Wanderers
2. Integrity Services of Maine
3. Richard Bader Physical Therapy
4. TK & Sons Concrete Foundations Inc.
5. Madison Avenue Associates

Once upon a time, deep in the forest, there was a beautiful, exotic flower garden. Inside this oasis of fragrant flowers, there lived two flowers named Rosy and Daisy.

They were friends who loved playing together. Each day, they would play their favorite game of "Tag the Flower."

On hazy days, these two blossoms would put on plays with their fair weather friends: the sun, clouds, and rain.

Each one helped the flowers continue to grow tall, healthy, and keep their dazzling colors.

One day, while they were getting ready to perform in a play with their fair weather friends, Rosy noticed a lime-colored sprout peeking out from the ground. For some reason, only one leaf, shaped like a half of a heart, was showing.

Rosy whispered to Daisy, "We cannot have this flower be in our *private* garden. She does not look like us. Someone must uproot her and plant this flower back into her *own* soil—you know, dirt made for *only* flowers like her!"

Deep down, Rosy was uncomfortable around all flowers who looked different from her. Even though Daisy didn't look like her either, Rosy and Daisy had grown up together. But having a new flower *invade* their garden was terrifying.

What if this new flower wanted to change the game rules? And what would she smell like? Would she be sweet? Or bitter . . . down to the roots?

Unlike Rosy, Daisy was a peacemaker, who kindly suggested, "Maybe once she comes up, she will at least act like us? I think we should wait until she blossoms. Then, we will be able to see what color she will be."

But sadly, Rosy thought that all new flowers should look exactly like her: be the same color and also have two leaves shaped like a heart.

A couple of days later, the new Calliandra flower erupted out of the soil, stretching out her newly grown stem and a single leaf. She was, indeed, a lovely, powder-puff, pink flower, with the nickname of Calli.

"Daisy, that does not count. You tagged my leaf, not my petal!" Calli heard much merriment at the other end of the garden. As her heart began to soar with excitement, Calli couldn't wait to introduce herself and join the fun!

"Hi, my name is Calli. This is my first day enjoying our beautiful garden. Will you teach me the game? It sounds like so much fun!"

Giggling, Daisy squealed with delight. "Sure, you can play with us! Trying to tag one of your petals, Calli, will be just like trying to grab a fairy's wing! Come on! Let me introduce you to—"

"No, Daisy, Calli cannot play with us," Rosy sternly interrupted. "She does not belong here.

She must be from **another** garden. Besides, she looks funny with only one leaf. It doesn't even look like a heart!"

Sadly, Calli walked off. *Will I ever fit in?* Calli wondered. *Am I from another garden . . . with only flowers that look just like me?*

However, there was one thing that bothered Calli. **Why did Rosy like Daisy? They were different types of flowers, too.**

The next day, as Calli watched and listened to Rosy and Daisy's laughter dance around the garden, she visited with the fair weather friends. Suddenly, Calli noticed that Rosy's eyes would disappear when she laughed; Rosy's eyes were just like hers.

Thinking out loud, Calli commented to her new fair weather friends, "I just don't understand why Rosy does not like me? We are all flowers! Each of us has a set of roots, a stem, a leaf or two, and flower petals. Who cares if one of us is a rose, a daisy, or another type of flower!"

Though the fair weather friends didn't speak, they silently floated back over to Rosy and Daisy.

Calli realized that her fair weather friends were sending
her a message: give the other flowers one more chance.
Besides, all flowers make mistakes from time to time.

Still laughing and giggling, Daisy and Rosy did not hear
Calli quietly walk over but felt a sudden warmth from
behind.

Turning around, they saw the fair weather friends surrounding Calli. Speechless, Daisy and Rosy waited for Calli to speak.

Gazing up at her friends from the sky gave Calli the courage to speak once again. "I know that some of us are from this garden while others were seeded in a distant land. I know that each of us have qualities that make us unique and beautiful. Rosy, you and I have eyes that are the same. And Daisy, we are both flowers, who have crazy petals like the sun's rays."

Calli continued, "I also admire your leaves and how they look like hearts. But . . . I have a real heart, too. How could I live if I didn't have one? Why can't we just accept each other for who we were created to be?"

All of the sudden, Rosy felt a **warm, happy tickle** begin to trickle onto her petals, down her stem, and right through her heart-shaped leaves.

Quickly, she realized that Calli was right. Flowers do come in different colors, shapes, and varieties. After all, this **was** the Gardener's original plan!

Because flowers are only around for a season, Rosy decided to waste no more time. Before the sun could sparkle once again, she asked Calli to join the flower gang and play their favorite game of "Tag the Flower." And you know what? Rosy realized that Daisy was right! Trying to tag one of Calli's petals was just like trying to grab a fairy's wing!

CPSIA information can be obtained
at www.ICGtesting.com
Printed in the USA
LVHW071727310120
645464LV00016B/1038